BOLDLY AND FE
LOVING

A Roadmap for Becoming a Man
After His Own Heart

AUTHOR
JOHN W. WILLIAMS JR

CONTENTS

INTRODUCTION

David is a model of devotion and passion for God. He showed that having a relationship with God is something to be celebrated and that devotion to Him should be put on full display. David had a fierce love for God that was evident in his actions such as worshipping, praying, meditating on the word, and dancing when the ark was returned. He was so filled with joy that the presence of God had returned, it was as though someone whom he had dearly loved and had been away had returned home. His longing, the desire of his heart had returned. He was not ashamed of his love for God and was willing to put his faith on full display, even when mocked by his wife Michal.

David's example of love for God is an example for us today. We are challenged to show the same level of devotion and willingness to put our faith on full display. We are called to love God with ferocity and joy and to not be ashamed of our faith. As we seek to follow in David's footsteps, may we be filled with the same level of passion and joy in our relationship with the Lord. Being a man after God's own heart has been the cry of my heart since I surrendered my heart to the Lord and I pray that it will become the cry of your heart and that this book will inspire you to love God with a Fervent Love.

God described David as being a man after His own heart, not because he was perfect or special but because he had a passionate love for God and God for him. They were in pursuit of each other. David's ferocious love for God shows us that it is okay to express our faith even in the face of ridicule or opposition. It also shows us that our relationship with God should be a priority and that we should love Him with full display. Let us strive to emulate David's example and be men and women after God's own heart.

CHAPTER 1

UNDERSTANDING FEROCIOUS LOVE

～

Defining Ferocious Love

In the pursuit of a deeper connection with our Creator, believers who love the Lord are often driven by an intense passion to experience His Love in its most powerful form. This subchapter aims to explore the concept of ferocious Love and its profound impact on our relationship with God. Ferocious Love is not an ordinary love; it is a love that burns with an unyielding fervor, allowing God's Love to overflow and permeate every aspect of our lives.

At its core, ferocious Love is an unquenchable thirst to know God intimately and to be known by Him. It is a love that compels us to seek His presence relentlessly, desiring to be wrapped in the warmth of His Love and guidance. This Love is not passive or lukewarm; it is a love that consumes us entirely, igniting a fire within our souls that cannot be extinguished.

When we love God with ferocious passion, we surrender ourselves completely to His will and purposes. It means placing Him above all else and allowing His Love to shape our thoughts, actions, and desires. Ferocious Love compels us to live a life fully surrendered to God, seeking

His guidance in every decision and allowing His Love to transform us from the inside out.

Ferocious Love is not limited to our personal relationship with God; it overflows and impacts every aspect of our lives. It prompts us to love others with the same intensity and selflessness that God has shown us. In our interactions with family, friends, and even strangers, ferocious Love compels us to extend grace, show compassion, and demonstrate the selfless Love of Christ.

In the pursuit of ferocious Love, we must also be willing to confront the areas in our lives where we may fall short. It requires us to examine our hearts, identify any barriers to Love, and surrender them to God. As we allow His Love to permeate every corner of our being, we can experience a transformation that empowers us to love as He loves.

Ferocious Love is a journey that requires commitment, sacrifice, and an unwavering desire to know God intimately. It is a love that surpasses human understanding and enables us to tap into the limitless depths of God's Love. So, let us embark on this journey together, believers who love the Lord and strive to love Him with ferocious passion, allowing His Love to overflow and impact every aspect of our lives.The Impact of Ferocious Love on Relationships

In our journey of loving God with intense passion and fervor, we inevitably come to realize the profound impact that ferocious Love has on our relationships. As believers who love the Lord, we understand that the essence of our faith lies in our ability to love others as He has loved us. And it is through ferocious Love that we can truly experience the transformative power of God's Love in our relationships.

Ferocious Love is not a timid or lukewarm affection; it is a love that burns brightly, consuming our hearts and overflowing into every aspect of our lives. When we allow God's Love to dwell within us, it becomes a force that defies all boundaries and expectations. It compels us to go above and beyond, to love unconditionally, and to show grace and forgiveness even in the face of adversity.

In our relationships with others, ferocious Love becomes a catalyst for healing, restoration, and growth. It breaks down walls of resentment and bitterness, replacing them with empathy and understanding. It teaches us to approach conflicts with humility and a desire for reconciliation rather than seeking to prove ourselves right.

Moreover, ferocious Love inspires us to serve others selflessly. It prompts us to look beyond our own needs and desires and consider the well-being of those around us. Whether it is through acts of kindness, words of encouragement, or simply being present for someone in their time of need, ferocious Love compels us to be intentional in our relationships.

But the impact of ferocious Love extends beyond just our immediate relationships. It has the power to influence and transform the world around us. When we love others with the same intensity and passion that God loves us, we become beacons of hope and light in a world that is often filled with darkness and despair.

Our ferocious Love becomes a testimony to the goodness and faithfulness of our Lord. It draws others closer to Him, inviting them to experience the same transformative Love that has captured our hearts. Through our relationships, we have the opportunity to reflect God's Love and bring about positive change in the lives of those we encounter.

In conclusion, the impact of ferocious Love on relationships is immeasurable. It has the power to heal wounds, build bridges, and ignite a passion for God in the hearts of others. As believers who love the Lord, let us continue to allow His ferocious Love to overflow from our lives, impacting every relationship we encounter and ultimately transforming the world around us.Surrendering to God's Ferocious Love

In this subchapter, we will explore the transformative power of surrendering to God's ferocious Love. For believers who love the Lord, there is a deep longing to experience an intense passion and fervor for God, allowing His Love to overflow and impact every aspect of life. This chapter aims to guide you towards surrendering completely to God's Love, inviting His ferocious Love to consume your heart, mind, and soul.

To surrender to God's ferocious Love means to let go of our own agendas, desires, and fears and instead yield to His divine will. It involves recognizing that His Love is all-encompassing and far greater than anything we can comprehend. Surrendering to His Love requires trust, faith, and a willingness to let Him take control.

One of the first steps in surrendering to God's ferocious Love is cultivating a deep intimacy with Him. This involves spending time in prayer, meditating on His Word, and seeking His presence. As we draw near to Him, our hearts become more aligned with His desires, and we begin to experience the overwhelming depth of His Love.

Surrendering to God's ferocious Love also means surrendering our own plans and dreams. It requires letting go of our need for control and submitting to His perfect timing and guidance. This can be challenging, as we often want to hold on to our own agendas. However, when we surrender to God's Love, we open ourselves up to His divine plan, which is always far greater and more fulfilling than anything we could have imagined.

Furthermore, surrendering to God's ferocious Love involves allowing His Love to impact every aspect of our lives. It means loving others with the same intensity and fervor that God loves us. His Love compels us to show kindness, compassion, and forgiveness to those around us. Surrendering to His Love enables us to see others through His eyes and extend grace and mercy, even when it is difficult.

In conclusion, surrendering to God's ferocious Love is a lifelong journey that requires constant surrender and a deepening relationship with Him. As believers who love the Lord, we are called to love Him with intense passion and fervor. By surrendering to His Love, we invite Him to transform our hearts, minds, and souls, allowing His Love to overflow and impact every aspect of our lives. May we continually surrender to God's ferocious Love and experience the abundant life and joy that comes from loving Him with our whole being.

CHAPTER 2

CULTIVATING A FEROCIOUS LOVE

∾

Developing a Passionate Prayer Life

In the journey of faith, prayer is not just a mere ritual or a religious duty to be fulfilled. It is an intimate conversation with the Almighty, a divine connection that has the power to transform lives. For believers who love the Lord, developing a passionate prayer life is essential to deepen their relationship with God and experience His overwhelming Love in every aspect of their existence.

To cultivate a passionate prayer life, one must first understand the significance of prayer. It is not merely a one-sided monologue, but a beautiful exchange of Love and affection between the Creator and His beloved creation. Prayer is an opportunity to pour out our hearts to God, to express our deepest joys, fears, and desires, knowing that He listens and responds. It is a sacred space where we can be vulnerable, honest, and transparent before the One who knows us intimately.

To develop a passionate prayer life, believers must prioritize consistent and intentional communication with God. Just as any relationship requires time and effort, so does our relationship with the Lord. Carving out specific moments of the day to spend in prayer, whether it be in the morning, during lunch breaks, or before bed, creates a rhythm that allows us to commune with God regularly.

In addition to consistency, the quality of our prayers matters. A passionate prayer life involves fervent and heartfelt prayers. It is not about reciting empty words or going through the motions, but about pouring out our souls before God with intensity and sincerity. It is about baring our deepest longings, dreams, and concerns before Him, trusting that He will respond with Love and wisdom.

Furthermore, developing a passionate prayer life requires an attitude of expectancy and faith. Believers must approach God with anticipation, knowing that He is a God who hears and answers prayers. It is the faith that moves mountains and brings about miracles in our lives. When we pray with passion and fervor, we align our desires with God's will, and His Love overflows into every aspect of our existence.

In conclusion, developing a passionate prayer life is a transformative journey that believers who love the Lord must embark upon. It is a commitment to consistent and intentional communication with God, pouring out our hearts with fervor and expectancy. As we develop this intimate connection with the Almighty, His Love will overflow into every aspect of our lives, transforming us into vessels of His intense affection. May we embrace this invitation to develop a passionate prayer life and experience the ferocious Love of God in its fullness. Engaging in Intimate Worship

As believers who love the Lord, our desire to express our intense passion and fervor for Him should extend beyond our daily lives and permeate every aspect of our existence. One powerful way to cultivate and demonstrate this ferocious Love is through engaging in intimate Worship.

Intimate Worship is more than just singing songs or attending church services. It is a heartfelt connection with our Creator, a sacred space where we pour out our adoration, awe, and love for Him. It is an opportunity to commune with God on a deep and personal level, allowing His Love to overflow into every area of our lives.

In intimate Worship, we are invited to come as we are, with all our joys, sorrows, victories, and failures. It is a safe place to lay down our burdens and find comfort in the presence of our Heavenly Father. As we surrender ourselves completely to Him, we create space for God to minister to our hearts, heal our wounds, and transform us from the inside out. I have gone into a worship service, jacked up and mixed up and came out fixed up with a heart that's filled up. There is a clarity that is experienced in the Lord's' presence.

Engaging in intimate Worship requires vulnerability and authenticity. It is not about putting on a show or going through the motions; it is about wholeheartedly giving ourselves to God. We must be willing to let go of our inhibitions, allowing His Love to penetrate the depths of our souls. It is in this place of vulnerability that we can experience the fullness of His Love and be transformed by His presence. We are literally transported from darkness to light, from the world's dominion into the kingdom of God's' beloved Son. Col 1:13

Intimate Worship also involves a deep reverence for God's holiness and a genuine desire to know Him more intimately. It is an act of surrender, acknowledging that He alone is worthy of our Worship and praise. As we draw near to Him, He draws near to us, revealing His character, His heart, and His desires for our lives. Seeing God is revelatory; it comes through revelation; the word says, "Without holiness, no man will see God, "sin puts a shroud over our spiritual eyes, almost like glaucoma causes dulled vision in those with the disease. Surrendering ourselves to the Lord and allowing him to purify our hearts is an act of Worship that opens the eyes of our hearts so that we can see Jesus.

When we engage in intimate Worship, we open ourselves up to the transformative power of God's Love. We become vessels through which His Love flows, impacting not only our lives but also the lives of those around us. Our ferocious passion for God becomes contagious, drawing others into a deeper relationship with Him.

In conclusion, engaging in intimate Worship is a vital component of loving God with a ferocious passion. It is an invitation to encounter the living God, to be transformed by His Love, and to overflow with His presence. May we continually seek opportunities to engage in intimate Worship, allowing His Love to impact every aspect of our lives and radiate through us to a world in need. Studying and Meditating on God's Word

As believers who love the Lord with a ferocious passion, it is essential for us to delve deep into the study and meditation of God's Word. The Bible is not just a collection of ancient texts; it is a living and breathing testament of God's Love and wisdom. It is through studying and meditating on His Word that we can truly grasp the depth of His affection for us and allow that Love to overflow into every aspect of our lives.

When we study God's Word, we are immersing ourselves in His truth and allowing it to transform our minds and hearts. It is through this process that we gain a deeper understanding of who God is and how He desires us to live. We discover His character, His promises, and His plans for our lives. Each word, each verse, and each chapter has the power to ignite a fire within us, leading us to a more intimate relationship with our Heavenly Father.

Meditation plays a crucial role in the study of God's Word. It is the practice of pondering and reflecting on the Scriptures, allowing them to permeate our thoughts and shape our perspectives. When we meditate on God's Word, we are creating space for the Holy Spirit to speak to us, to reveal hidden truths, and to guide us in our daily walk with Him. It is through meditation that the words on the page become a personal and life-giving message from God to our souls.

Studying and meditating on God's Word is not a mere intellectual exercise; it is an act of devotion and Love. It is an intentional and disciplined pursuit of God's heart. As believers who love the Lord with a ferocious passion, we recognize the power of His Word to transform our lives and the lives of those around us. We eagerly consume His Word, hungering for more of His presence and desiring to align our lives with His perfect will.

In conclusion, studying and meditating on God's Word is a vital component of our journey of ferocious Love for Him. It is through this practice that we deepen our understanding of His Love and allow it to overflow into every aspect of our lives. As we immerse ourselves in His Word, we are transformed from the inside out, becoming vessels of His Love and light in a world desperately in need of Him. Let us, therefore, commit ourselves to the study and meditation of God's Word, allowing His truth to shape us into passionate and fervent disciples who reflect His Love to the world.

CHAPTER 3
FEROCIOUS LOVE IN ACTION

〰

Loving God with All our Heart, Mind, and Soul

In this subchapter, we delve into the concept of loving God with every fiber of our being. As believers who already love the Lord, we understand the importance of nurturing a deep relationship with Him. However, it is crucial to take our Love for God to the next level, experiencing a love that is intense, passionate, and fervent. This chapter explores the idea of ferocious Love, where our affection for God overflows and impacts every aspect of our lives.

Loving God with all our heart, mind, and soul is not merely a suggestion but a commandment from the Lord Himself. It is the foundation upon which our entire spiritual journey is built. By dedicating our hearts, minds, and souls to God, we align ourselves with His divine purpose and find ultimate fulfillment in Him.

To truly love God with ferocious passion, we must first examine our hearts. Our heart is the seat of our emotions and desires, and it is here that our Love for God must reside. We must ask ourselves, "Do I love God with all my heart? Do I desire Him above all else? Are my affections fully devoted to Him?" Only when our heart is wholly surrendered to God can we experience the depth of His Love and allow it to overflow into every aspect of our lives.

Next, we must engage our minds in the pursuit of loving God. Our mind is the faculty through which we understand and perceive the things of God. We must continuously renew our minds through studying His Word, meditating on His promises, and seeking His wisdom. By filling our minds with the knowledge of God, we equip ourselves to love Him more deeply and to discern His will for our lives.

Lastly, loving God with all our souls involves surrendering our entire being to Him. Our soul encompasses our spirit, will, and emotions. It is through our soul that we experience intimacy with God. By surrendering our will to Him, allowing Him to guide our decisions, and aligning our emotions with His truth, we open ourselves up to a love that transcends human understanding.

As believers who love the Lord, let us commit to loving Him with ferocious passion. May our hearts overflow with Love, our minds be renewed with His truth, and our souls be fully surrendered to Him. In doing so, we will experience the transformative power of His Love in every aspect of our lives. Serving Others with Ferocious Love

As believers who love the Lord, our journey of faith is not just about our personal relationship with God. It is also about how we express that Love and passion for Him in our daily interactions with others. The subchapter titled "Serving Others with Ferocious Love" delves into the profound impact of allowing God's Love to overflow from our hearts and impact every aspect of our lives.

Ferocious Love is not a passive or lukewarm affection; it is an intense passion and fervor that compels us to action. It is a love that cannot be contained but spills over into the lives of those around us. When we truly grasp the depth of God's Love for us and experience the transformation it brings, we cannot help but be moved to serve others with the same ferocity.

Serving others with a ferocious Love means going beyond mere acts of kindness or fulfilling obligations. It is a radical mindset shift that compels us to see every person we encounter as someone deserving of Love, compassion, and grace. It means stepping out of our comfort zones, reaching out to the marginalized and forgotten, and meeting the needs of those around us, whether physical, emotional, or spiritual.

But serving others with ferocious Love goes even deeper than mere acts of service. It requires us to embrace vulnerability, humility, and selflessness. It means laying aside our own desires and agendas to prioritize the needs of others. It means seeking to understand and empathize with their struggles, offering a listening ear, and extending a helping hand.

When we serve others with ferocious Love, we become vessels of God's Love in the world. Our actions become a tangible expression of His Love, mercy, and compassion. People should be able to witness the transformative power of God's Love through us as we reflect His character and extend His grace.

Ultimately, serving others with ferocious Love is an act of Worship. It is an offering of ourselves to God, as we imitate His sacrificial Love and seek to bring His kingdom on earth. It is a way to demonstrate our gratitude for all He has done for us and to participate in His redemptive work in the world.

May this subchapter inspire believers who love the Lord to embrace ferocious Love and allow it to overflow into every aspect of their lives. May it encourage them to serve others with a passion that reflects God's heart, transforming lives and bringing glory to His name. Sharing God's Love with the World

As believers who love the Lord, our commitment to living a life of intense affection for God should not be confined to our personal relationship with Him. Our Love for God should overflow and impact every aspect of our lives, including our interactions with others and our responsibility to share His Love with the world.

In this subchapter, titled "Sharing God's Love with the World," we explore the profound significance of spreading God's Love to those around us. When we experience the ferocious passion and fervor of loving God, it becomes impossible to keep His Love to ourselves. His Love compels us to share it with others, to become vessels through which His Love can flow.

Sharing God's Love is not a mere suggestion; it is a commandment that Jesus Himself emphasized throughout His ministry. In Matthew 22:37-40, Jesus proclaimed that the greatest commandment is to love God with all our heart, soul, and mind, and the second is to love our neighbors as ourselves. These two commandments are inseparable, as loving God deeply naturally leads us to love others unconditionally.

When we share God's Love with the world, we become instruments of transformation. The impact of His Love on our lives is so powerful that it has the potential to change the lives of those we encounter. By embodying His Love, we can be a beacon of hope to a broken and hurting world. Our actions, words, and attitudes should reflect His Love, serving as a testament to the transformative power of a relationship with Him.

Sharing God's Love goes beyond mere acts of kindness or charity; it is about introducing people to the source of all Love and redemption. It is about pointing others to Jesus, who is the embodiment of God's Love. Through our genuine Love and compassion, we can draw others closer to Him, inviting them into a relationship that will forever change their lives.

As believers who love the Lord, let us embrace the call to share God's Love with the world. Let us allow His Love to overflow from our lives, impacting every aspect of our existence. May our ferocious passion for God drive us to love others intensely and fervently, just as He loves us. In doing so, we become conduits of His Love, spreading His light and transforming the world one heart at a time.

CHAPTER 4

OVERCOMING OBSTACLES TO FEROCIOUS LOVE

∼

Dealing with Doubt and Fear

In the journey of faith, it is natural for believers who love the Lord to encounter moments of doubt and fear. These emotions can arise unexpectedly, causing uncertainty and questioning in our hearts. However, it is crucial to recognize that doubt and fear do not define our faith but rather present opportunities for growth and deeper intimacy with God. In this subchapter, we will explore practical ways to overcome doubt and fear, allowing our ferocious Love for God to prevail in every aspect of our lives.

First and foremost, it is essential to acknowledge that doubt is a normal part of the human experience. Even the most devout believers have wrestled with doubt at some point. Instead of suppressing or ignoring these doubts, we must face them head-on. Bringing our questions and concerns before God, we can seek His wisdom and guidance, trusting that He will provide clarity and understanding. It is through these moments of doubt that our faith can be refined and strengthened.

Fear, on the other hand, often stems from a lack of trust in God's sovereignty and goodness. As believers, we need to remind ourselves of God's faithfulness throughout history and in our own lives. By meditating on His promises and spending time in His Word, we can find comfort and assurance in His unfailing Love. Additionally, surrounding ourselves with a supportive community of believers who can offer encouragement and prayer can help alleviate our fears.

To overcome doubt and fear, we must also cultivate a lifestyle of Worship and gratitude. By continually focusing our hearts and minds on God's goodness, we can shift our perspective from our doubts and fears to His power and provision. Engaging in fervent prayer, worshipping through music, and immersing ourselves in Scripture can all contribute to a heart filled with ferocious Love for God, leaving little room for doubt and fear.

Lastly, it is essential to remember that doubt and fear are not signs of weakness but opportunities for growth. Embracing these emotions with humility and a desire to seek God's truth can lead to a deeper understanding of His character and purposes. As believers who love the Lord, we are called to walk by faith, trusting that He will lead us through every season of doubt and fear, strengthening us along the way.

In conclusion, the journey of faith is not without its challenges. Doubt and fear may arise, but as believers who love the Lord, we have the tools to overcome these obstacles. By facing our doubts, trusting in God's faithfulness, surrounding ourselves with a supportive community, and cultivating a lifestyle of Worship, we can navigate through doubt and fear with ferocious Love for God. Let us embrace these moments as opportunities for growth and deeper intimacy with our Heavenly Father, knowing that He is with us every step of the way. Letting Go of Past Hurts and Forgiving

In our journey of intense affection and fervent Love for the Lord, one of the most important steps we must take is letting go of past hurts and forgiving. As believers who love the Lord, we understand the power of His Love and how it can transform our lives. However, to fully experience the overflowing impact of His Love in every aspect of our lives, we must learn to release the burdens of the past and extend forgiveness to those who have wronged us.

Holding onto past hurts can be like carrying a heavy load on our backs, weighing us down and preventing us from moving forward. It hinders our ability to fully embrace the Love and grace of God. But as followers of Christ, we are called to live a different way. We are called to imitate the Love and forgiveness that God has shown us.

Forgiveness is not always easy, but it is a necessary step in our spiritual growth. When we choose to forgive, we are not excusing the actions of others or denying the pain they have caused us. Instead, we are acknowledging our own humanity and extending the same grace and mercy that God has shown us. By releasing the grip of past hurts, we create space for God's Love to flow freely in our hearts.

Moreover, forgiveness is not a one-time event. It is a continuous process that requires patience and perseverance. We may need to forgive the same person multiple times or work through layers of pain. But each act of forgiveness brings us closer to the heart of God and allows His Love to penetrate deeper into our souls.

As believers who love the Lord with ferocious passion, we must also remember that forgiveness is not just for our own benefit. It is a testimony to the world of God's transforming power. When we let go of past hurts and forgive, we demonstrate the radical Love of Christ that surpasses all understanding.

In conclusion, letting go of past hurts and forgiving is a crucial aspect of living a life of intense affection for God. We must release the burdens of the past, extend forgiveness to those who have wronged us, and continually choose to imitate the Love and forgiveness that God has shown us. By doing so, we create space for God's Love to overflow and impact every aspect of our lives. Let us embrace the power of forgiveness and experience the freedom and joy that comes from loving God with a ferocious passion. Battling Distractions and Prioritizing God's Love

In this fast-paced and ever-distracting world, it can be challenging for believers who love the Lord to maintain a steadfast focus on Him. Our days are filled with endless distractions, pulling us away from our relationship with God and causing us to lose sight of His intense Love for us. However, it is crucial that we learn to battle these distractions and prioritize God's Love above all else.

To truly love God with ferocious passion, we must first recognize the power of His Love for us. God's Love is not a mere emotion or sentiment; it is a force that can transform our lives. When we understand the depth and intensity of His Love, we cannot help but be captivated by it. It becomes our driving force, the very essence of our existence.

However, distractions often come disguised as important tasks or responsibilities. We find ourselves consumed by the demands of our careers, relationships, and personal ambitions, leaving little time or energy for cultivating our relationship with God. It is crucial that we learn to discern the difference between what is truly important and what is merely a distraction.

One practical way to battle distractions is to establish daily rhythms of seeking God's presence. This can include setting aside specific times for prayer, meditating on, and reading His Word. By prioritizing these moments, we create space for God to speak to us and for His Love to overflow into every aspect of our lives.

Another key aspect of battling distractions is guarding our hearts and minds. We live in a world that bombards us with information, opinions, and ideologies that are often contrary to God's truth. By immersing ourselves in His Word and surrounding ourselves with like-minded believers, we can protect our hearts from being swayed by worldly influences.

Furthermore, it is important to cultivate a spirit of surrender and submission to God's will. When we align our priorities with Him, we are better equipped to navigate the distractions that come our way. By constantly reminding ourselves of His Love and surrendering our desires to Him, we can live a life that is fueled by a ferocious passion for Him.

In conclusion, as believers who love the Lord, we must be intentional in battling distractions and prioritizing God's Love. By recognizing the power of His Love, establishing daily rhythms of seeking His presence, guarding our hearts and minds, and surrendering to His will, we can experience the fullness of ferocious Love. Let us determine to love God with intense passion and fervor, allowing His Love to overflow and impact every aspect of our lives.

CHAPTER 5

DEEPENING OUR FEROCIOUS LOVE

~

Embracing God's Grace and Mercy

In the journey of intense affection and fervent Love for God, believers who love the Lord must understand the significance of embracing God's grace and mercy. These two divine attributes are fundamental to our relationship with Him and play a pivotal role in our spiritual growth and transformation. As we delve deeper into the realms of ferocious Love, we must allow the overflowing Love of God to impact every aspect of our lives, and in doing so, we must learn to fully embrace His grace and mercy.

God's grace is the unmerited favor that He extends to us, granting forgiveness and salvation through faith in Jesus Christ. We, as believers, have been redeemed by His grace and are no longer held captive by our past mistakes and sins. It is through His grace that we are justified and made righteous in His sight. However, we must not take this grace for granted but rather cherish it as a precious gift that continually transforms us. Grace does not make us weaker and more sinful but stronger; it is the power given by God to do a thing, a divine ability. When you say I am under grace, you are saying I am strong. When Paul was going through a difficult time, he prayed for deliverance, and God told him my grace is sufficient for you. He was was not telling Paul no, he was telling Paul that I have given you the ability to endure and go through. Whatever Paul was going through was difficult and apparently part of his call, and he needed to go through instead of getting out of the situation; grace helps us to get or go through. God does not despise us or forsake us when we are weak, he strengthens us and receives glory when he empowers weak people to do great things. 2 Corinthians 12:9

In our pursuit of loving God with intense passion and fervor, we must also embrace His mercy. God's mercy is His compassionate response to our weaknesses, failures, and struggles. It is in His mercy that He withholds the punishment we rightfully deserve and instead extends His loving kindness towards us. It is through His mercy that we find comfort and strength, knowing that He understands our human frailties and offers us a fresh start each day. Lamentation 3:22-23

As believers, we need to remind ourselves constantly of the grace and mercy that God has lavished upon us. This understanding enables us to extend grace and mercy to others, just as Christ has done for us. By embracing God's grace and mercy, our ferocious Love for Him becomes a catalyst for transformation in our relationships, communities, and the world.

Let us not forget that it is through the grace and mercy of God that we are able to experience the fullness of His Love. As we surrender ourselves to Him, allowing His

Love to overflow, we will witness the transformative power of grace and mercy in our lives. We will become vessels of His Love, radiating His grace and mercy to a broken world that is in desperate need of His redemptive Love.

In conclusion, embracing God's grace and mercy is not only essential but transformative in our journey of intense affection and fervent Love for Him. Let us allow His grace to continually shape us and His mercy to empower us as we love Him with a ferocious passion. May we be vessels of His Love, extending His grace and mercy to all those around us, and may our lives be a testament to the power of His Love in every aspect of our existence. Growing in Intimacy with the Holy Spirit

As believers who love the Lord, our ultimate desire is to grow in our intimacy with Him. We long to experience His presence in a profound and life-transforming way. One of the most powerful ways to cultivate and deepen this intimacy is by nurturing a close relationship with the Holy Spirit.

The Holy Spirit, the third person of the Trinity, is not just a distant and mysterious force. He is our constant companion, the one who dwells within us, guiding, empowering, and transforming us. He is the tangible expression of God's Love and power in our lives, and developing a deeper connection with Him is essential for our spiritual growth.

To grow in intimacy with the Holy Spirit, we must first acknowledge His presence and importance in our lives. We need to recognize Him as a person, not just a concept or an abstract idea. The Holy Spirit is our counselor, comforter, and advocate. He longs to lead us into all truth, reveal the deep things of God, and empower us to live a life that reflects Christ's Love.

Intimacy with the Holy Spirit is nurtured through prayer and Worship. As we set aside dedicated time to seek His presence, we open our hearts to His leading and direction. We invite Him to speak to us, to reveal His heart, and to transform us from the inside out. In the stillness of prayer, we learn to listen to His gentle whisper and allow His Love to penetrate every aspect of our lives.

Furthermore, growing in intimacy with the Holy Spirit requires a posture of surrender and yieldedness. We must be willing to let go of our own desires, plans, and agendas, and submit to His will. We invite Him to take full control of our lives, allowing His Love to overflow and impact every area, be it our relationships, work, or ministry. This surrender is not passive; it is an active pursuit of His presence and an ongoing commitment to walk in step with Him. I have learned in my own life that the quicker I surrender to the Holy Spirit, the more I experience his presence, if he convicts you of sin, repent quickly, if he moves on you to do a thing, do it quickly, if he says come away with me, surrender and worship him quickly and his presence will intensify, and our spiritual hunger will also intensify. When we pursue the Lord, he will pursues us, James 4:8

As we grow in intimacy with the Holy Spirit, our Love for God becomes more ferocious and passionate. His Love, flowing through us, impacts every aspect of our lives, transforming us into vessels of His grace, mercy, and power. Our desire to love Him and others intensifies, and our lives become a reflection of His Love in a world that desperately needs it.

In conclusion, growing in intimacy with the Holy Spirit is not a one-time event, but an ongoing journey. It requires intentional effort, a hunger for His presence, and a willingness to surrender to His leading. As believers who love the Lord, let us seek to cultivate this intimacy, allowing His Love to overflow and impact every aspect of our lives. May our ferocious passion for Him ignite a fire within us that cannot be quenched, and may we become beacons of His Love in a world longing for intimacy with its Creator. Experiencing the Overflow of God's Love in our lives

As believers who love the Lord, we are called to embrace a life filled with intense affection for God. This ferocious passion stems from a deep understanding and experience of God's overflowing Love in our lives. When we allow His Love to impact every aspect of our existence, we can truly live a life that reflects His character and purpose.

31

The concept of experiencing the overflow of God's Love is not merely an abstract idea or a distant theological concept. It is a tangible reality that we can encounter daily. It is a love that surpasses all understanding, a love that is relentless and unchanging, a love that transforms us from the inside out. Obedience is a result of being in Love with God, it's what drives a true believer. When you met the Love of your life, you showered them with gifts and longed to be with the one you loved; no one had to force you to come and see your beloved; in fact, your days went by faster in anticipation of seeing the one you loved. Our Love for God should move us with that same kind of intensity, that first love intensity, that says I will do anything to make you happy, to bless you. You are not doing those things to get the person to love you but because you are loved and you want to love in return. God loves us; we never have to question that. Jesus demonstrated it when he stretched out his hands on the cross. There is no greater love than to lay down your life for someone. His Love is not transactional: do this or do that, and then I will love you; we don't have to pay for his Love; he gives it freely; we don't have to earn it or be perfect to receive it; he died for us when we were sinners when we were all messed up. John 14:15, John 15:13

When we open our hearts to receive this Love, we become vessels for its overflow. Just as a cup cannot contain more than its capacity, our hearts cannot contain the boundless Love of God. It spills over, impacting our thoughts, actions, and relationships. It becomes the driving force behind our ferocious Love for God and others.

Allowing God's Love to overflow in our lives requires surrender and vulnerability. It means relinquishing control and allowing His Love to permeate every area of our being. It means letting go of our own agendas and desires and embracing His will for our lives. In doing so, we experience a profound intimacy with our Creator, a connection that goes beyond our understanding.

When we live in the overflow of God's Love, we become conduits of His grace and mercy. We extend Love to others not out of obligation or duty but out of a genuine desire to share the Love that has been lavished upon us. Our relationships are transformed as we learn to forgive, show kindness, and extend grace, just as God has done for us.

Experiencing the overflow of God's Love in our lives also empowers us to overcome the challenges and trials we may face. It gives us hope in the midst of despair, strength in times of weakness, and peace in moments of chaos. We can rest assured that His Love will never fail us, and His presence will sustain us through every storm.

In conclusion, as believers who love the Lord, our goal should be to experience the overflow of God's Love in our lives. It is through this intense affection and ferocious passion that we can truly love God with all our hearts, allowing His Love to impact every aspect of our existence. May we continually seek His presence, surrender to His Love, and become vessels of His overflow in a world that desperately needs to encounter His relentless Love.

CHAPTER 6
SUSTAINING FEROCIOUS LOVE

〜

Nurturing a Strong Faith Foundation

As believers who love the Lord, we understand the importance of building a strong faith foundation. Our journey of faith is not a one-time event but a continuous process of growth and deepening our relationship with God. Just like a house needs a solid foundation to stand tall against the storms, our faith requires a strong foundation to withstand the challenges and trials of life.

To nurture a strong faith foundation, we must first cultivate an intense passion and fervor for God. This ferocious Love for Him must overflow from our hearts and impact every aspect of our lives. It is not enough to simply love God; we must love Him with all our heart, soul, mind, and strength. This kind of Love compels us to seek Him wholeheartedly, hunger for His presence, and surrender our lives completely to His will.

One of the key ways to nurture a strong faith foundation is through a consistent and intimate relationship with God. This means setting aside dedicated time each day for prayer, Worship, and studying His Word. We must prioritize our relationship with Him above all else and make it the foundation upon which we build our lives. As we spend time in His presence, we will experience His Love, receive His guidance, and be empowered by His Spirit.

Another vital aspect of nurturing a strong faith foundation is being actively involved in a Christ-centered community. Surrounding ourselves with other believers who share our passion for God creates an environment of encouragement, accountability, and growth. Together, we can learn from one another, support each other in times of need, and spur one another on toward Love and good deeds.

Additionally, we must continually deepen our understanding of God's Word and theological truths. This requires a commitment to lifelong learning and a hunger for truth. By studying the Bible, reading books by trusted authors, and engaging in theological discussions, we can strengthen our faith and guard against false teachings.

Lastly, nurturing a strong faith foundation involves living out our faith in practical ways. As believers, we are called to be the hands and feet of Jesus, showing His Love and compassion to a hurting world. This means actively serving others, demonstrating forgiveness and grace, and living a life that reflects the character of Christ.

In conclusion, nurturing a strong faith foundation is essential for believers who love the Lord. By cultivating an intense passion for God, prioritizing our relationship with Him, actively participating in a Christ-centered community, deepening our understanding of His Word, and living out our faith in practical ways, we can build a firm foundation that will withstand the storms of life. Let us pursue this ferocious Love for God, allowing His Love to overflow and impact every aspect of our lives.

Surrounding Ourselves with Like-minded Believers.

In the quest to love God with ferocious passion, it is crucial to surround ourselves with like-minded believers. As believers who love the Lord, we understand the importance of cultivating an environment that nurtures and strengthens our faith. This subchapter explores the significance of surrounding ourselves with individuals who share our intense affection for God and how it can impact every aspect of our lives.

When we surround ourselves with like-minded believers, we create a community that encourages and supports our spiritual growth. These individuals understand the depth of our Love for God because they, too, have experienced it in their own lives. We can share our struggles, victories, and questions without fear of judgment or misunderstanding. Together, we can spur one another on to love and good deeds, consistently reminding each other of the fervor with which we should pursue our relationship with God.

Moreover, surrounding ourselves with like-minded believers provides a sense of accountability. They can help us stay on track in our devotion to God and challenge us to live out our faith in practical ways. By sharing our lives with those who also have a ferocious love for God, we are less likely to compromise our beliefs or be swayed by the world's distractions. This accountability ensures that our passion for God remains at the forefront of our lives and impacts every aspect of our actions, decisions, and relationships.

Additionally, being part of a community of like-minded believers offers a unique opportunity for growth and learning. We can engage in deep discussions, study the Word together, and share insights that deepen our understanding of God's Love. In these interactions, we are stretched, challenged, and inspired to love God more passionately. We can learn from one another's experiences, testimonies, and wisdom, broadening our perspective and enriching our faith journey.

Ultimately, surrounding ourselves with like-minded believers allows us to experience the fullness of God's Love. As we love God with ferocious passion, His Love overflows into every aspect of our lives. The community of believers becomes a vessel through which God's Love is demonstrated and experienced tangibly. It is a place where we find encouragement, strength, and inspiration to continue loving God relentlessly.

In conclusion, for believers who love the Lord with intense passion and fervor, surrounding ourselves with like-minded believers is essential. It creates a nurturing environment for our faith to grow, provides accountability, and offers opportunities for learning and growth. Let us actively seek out and invest in relationships with those who share our intense affection for God as we strive to love Him with all our hearts, souls, and minds. Continuously Seeking God's Presence

Subchapter: Continuously Seeking God's Presence

Introduction: In our journey as believers who love the Lord with a ferocious passion, it is vital to seek God's presence continuously. This subchapter delves into the significance of pursuing an intimate relationship with our Heavenly Father, allowing His Love to overflow and impact every aspect of our lives.

1. The Desire for Deeper Intimacy: As believers who love the Lord, we are driven by an intense affection for Him. This affection fuels our desire to know Him intimately and experience His presence in our lives. It is through seeking God's presence that we can cultivate a deeper connection with Him.

2. Developing a Lifestyle of Seeking: Seeking God's presence isn't a one-time event; it is a consistent, lifelong pursuit. It involves setting aside dedicated time for prayer, Worship, and studying His Word. By making seeking God a

priority in our daily lives, we position ourselves to encounter His Love and experience His power.

3. The Rewards of Seeking God: When we seek God's presence with a fervent heart, we are rewarded with a deeper understanding of His character and His will for our lives. Through seeking Him, we gain wisdom, guidance, and supernatural peace that surpasses all understanding. When we pursue God, we get to experience his presence. When we marinade in his presence, we are changed, and we come out of his presence with a tangible anointing, and others are changed. When we marinade, we are permeated with God's presence. When meat is marinated, it takes on the flavor of the marinade. What you marinade in becomes part of you. If you marinade chicken in teriyaki sauce, we don't just call it chicken any longer, we call it teriyaki chicken. We become more like Jesus in his presence.

4. Overcoming Distractions and Obstacles: In our fast-paced world, distractions and obstacles can hinder our ability to seek God's presence. However, as believers who love the Lord, we must be intentional about overcoming these challenges. This could involve setting boundaries, fasting, and seeking accountability from fellow believers.

5.   The Power of God's Presence: When we continuously seek God's presence, we position ourselves to experience His transformative power. His presence brings healing, deliverance, and restoration to our lives. It is in His presence that our ferocious Love for Him is ignited and sustained.

Conclusion: As believers who love the Lord with ferocious passion, seeking God's presence is an essential aspect of our relationship with Him. It is through this continuous seeking that we deepen our intimacy with Him, allowing His Love to overflow and impact every aspect of our lives. May we never tire of pursuing His presence and experiencing the fullness of His Love and power.

CHAPTER 7

FEROCIOUS LOVE IN EVERY ASPECT OF LIFE

∼

Ferocious Love in Marriage and Family

In the journey of intense affection towards God, believers who love the Lord often find themselves yearning for their relationships with their spouses and families to be equally infused with ferocious Love. They desire to experience the overflow of God's Love in every aspect of their lives, including their marriages and families. This subchapter explores the transformative power of ferocious Love within the context of marriage and family, illuminating how it can elevate these relationships to new heights.

Marriage, a sacred bond ordained by God, serves as a fertile ground for ferocious Love to flourish. It is an opportunity to mirror God's Love for His people, selflessly giving and sacrificially serving one another. Ferocious Love in marriage is not merely an emotion or a fleeting feeling; it is a commitment to consistently choose Love and to seek the well-being of one's spouse continuously. It is a love that endures through the storms of life, strengthens during hardships, and celebrates the joys together. By loving our spouses with intensity and fervor, we demonstrate the tangible presence of God's Love in our lives.

Similarly, ferocious Love plays a crucial role in shaping the dynamics of a family. It creates an environment where Love is not just spoken but lived out daily. Within the family unit, ferocious Love fosters mutual respect, forgiveness, and unity. It encourages parents to raise their children with godly principles, disciplining with Love and nurturing their spiritual growth. It inspires siblings to cultivate deep bonds, supporting and encouraging one another through life's trials. Through ferocious Love, families become a reflection of God's Love, radiating His grace, mercy, and compassion to the world.

Practicing ferocious Love in marriage and family requires intentional effort and a reliance on God's strength. It necessitates prioritizing time with God individually and as a family, seeking His guidance and wisdom in all decisions. It involves recognizing and addressing personal shortcomings, extending grace and forgiveness to one another, and continuously striving for growth in Love. It also entails creating an atmosphere of open communication where each individual feels heard, valued, and loved.

Believers who love the Lord and seek to live out ferocious Love in their marriages and families will undoubtedly experience transformational blessings. As they allow God's Love to overflow and impact every aspect of their lives, they will witness their relationships flourishing with an intensity that can only come from the divine. May this subchapter inspire and encourage believers to pursue ferocious Love in their marriages and families, becoming a radiant testimony of God's Love and faithfulness in their lives. Ferocious Love in the Workplace

In today's fast-paced and competitive world, it can be challenging to maintain our faith and commitment to the Lord in the workplace. However, as believers who love the Lord, we have the incredible opportunity to demonstrate His Love and character even in the most mundane tasks or high-pressure environments. This subchapter, titled "Ferocious Love in the Workplace," explores how we can love God with intense passion and fervor, allowing His Love to overflow and impact every aspect of our professional lives.

The workplace often becomes a battleground for our faith, where temptations, conflicts, and ethical dilemmas arise. However, it is precisely in these moments that our ferocious Love for God can shine the brightest. By surrendering our work to Him and seeking His guidance daily, we can transform our workplace into a space where His Love is evident in our words, actions, and relationships.

First and foremost, loving God fervently means seeking to honor Him in all that we do. Whether we are employees or employers, we can choose to conduct ourselves with integrity, honesty, and excellence. Our commitment to excellence not only reflects our dedication to our jobs but also our desire to bring glory to God. By being diligent and hardworking, we become living testimonies of God's Love and faithfulness.

Furthermore, ferocious Love in the workplace means treating our colleagues with kindness, respect, and compassion. We have the opportunity to be a source of encouragement and support to those around us, lending a listening ear or offering a helping hand when needed. When we demonstrate Love in our interactions, we create an environment that fosters unity, collaboration, and growth.

Additionally, our ferocious Love for God can be displayed through our willingness to share the good news of the Gospel with our coworkers. By living out our faith authentically and being open about our beliefs, we create opportunities for others to witness the transformative power of God's Love in our lives. Through our actions and words, we become conduits of His Love, guiding others towards a personal relationship with Him.

In conclusion, "Ferocious Love in the Workplace" is a call to believers who love the Lord to carry His Love into their professional lives. By seeking to honor God, treating others with kindness and compassion, and sharing the Gospel, we can impact our workplaces with His Love and transform them into environments where

His presence is evident. Let us embrace the opportunity to love God with intense passion and fervor, allowing His Love to overflow and touch every aspect of our lives, including our careers. Ferocious Love in Ministry and Serving Others

As believers who love the Lord, our journey of faith is not just about personal devotion and experiencing God's Love in our own lives. It is also about sharing that Love with others and serving them with ferocious passion and intensity. This subchapter on "Ferocious Love in Ministry and Serving Others" explores the transformative power of Love and how it can impact every aspect of our lives.

Ministry is not limited to pastors, missionaries, or those who work in full-time church roles. It is a calling for every believer to serve others selflessly and sacrificially, motivated by an intense affection for God. When we tap into the ferocious Love of God, it becomes a driving force that propels us to reach out to those in need, both within and outside the church community.

Ferocious Love in ministry goes beyond fulfilling religious obligations or checking off a to-do list. It is a deep and intense passion that compels us to go the extra mile, to love others unconditionally, and to meet their needs with a servant's heart. It means being willing to step out of our comfort zones and embrace the messiness of people's lives, just as Jesus did during His earthly ministry.

When we allow God's Love to overflow in our lives, it becomes contagious. Our actions and attitudes become a reflection of His Love, drawing others to Him. It is through our acts of kindness, compassion, and service that we become conduits of God's grace and mercy, impacting the lives of those around us.

Ferocious Love in ministry also requires us to be intentional about cultivating healthy relationships within the body of Christ. It means fostering a community where Love and unity prevail, where we encourage and support one another in our spiritual journeys. By loving and serving one another fervently, we create an environment where God's Love can flourish and transform lives.

In conclusion, embracing ferocious Love in ministry and serving others is not a mere addendum to our faith; it is at the very core of what it means to follow Christ. As believers who love the Lord, let us allow His Love to overflow in our lives, impacting every aspect of our existence. May our Love for Him compel us to serve others with intensity, selflessness, and unwavering devotion, reflecting His Love to a world in desperate need.

CHAPTER 8

THE TRANSFORMATIVE POWER OF FEROCIOUS LOVE

~

Healing and Restoration through Ferocious Love

In our journey of loving God with intense passion and fervor, we often overlook the immense power of His Love to heal and restore every aspect of our lives. We, as believers who love the Lord, need to grasp the concept of ferocious Love and allow it to overflow from our hearts, impacting our relationships, emotions, physical well-being, and spiritual growth.

When we talk about ferocious Love, we are not referring to a love that is gentle or mild. Instead, it is a love that is fearless, relentless, and unstoppable. It is a love that pursues us in our brokenness, heals our deepest wounds, and restores us to wholeness.

In the realm of relationships, ferocious Love transforms how we interact with others. It pushes us beyond the boundaries of our comfort zones, teaching us to love even those who have hurt us. It enables us to forgive and reconcile, opening doors to restoration and unity. This Love compels us to serve selflessly, without expecting anything in return, and to extend grace to those who don't deserve it.

Emotionally, ferocious Love brings healing and restoration to our wounded souls. It enables us to embrace our vulnerabilities, allowing God's Love to mend the broken pieces of our hearts. It brings comfort in times of sorrow, joy in times of despair, and hope in times of darkness. This Love empowers us to overcome fear, anxiety, and depression, as we trust in the unfailing Love of our Heavenly Father. Hebrews 13:5

Physically, ferocious Love impacts our well-being. It encourages us to take care of our bodies, recognizing that they are temples of the Holy Spirit. This Love motivates us to make healthy choices, nourishing ourselves with proper nutrition, exercise, and rest. It also inspires us to extend this Love to others, caring for their physical needs and promoting their well-being.

Spiritually, ferocious Love propels us into a deeper relationship with God. It compels us to seek Him passionately, to hunger and thirst for His presence. This Love ignites the fire within us, creating a burning desire to know Him more intimately and to live in obedience to His Word. It enables us to surrender our lives completely, allowing God's Love to transform us from the inside out.

Dear believers who love the Lord, let us embrace ferocious Love with open hearts and allow it to permeate every aspect of our lives. As we do so, we will experience healing and restoration beyond our wildest dreams. We will become vessels of God's Love, impacting the world around us and drawing others into the transformative power of His ferocious Love.Finding Purpose and Fulfillment in God's Love

As believers who love the Lord, we understand the importance of seeking purpose and fulfillment in our lives. We yearn to experience a deep connection with God, allowing His Love to transform every aspect of our existence. In this subchapter, we will explore the profound impact of finding purpose and fulfillment in God's Love, and how it can ignite within us a ferocious passion for Him.

When we truly grasp the magnitude of God's Love for us, it becomes the driving force behind our desire to live a purposeful life. His Love is not just a mere sentiment or emotion; it is a powerful, life-changing force that can propel us towards our destiny. As we immerse ourselves in His Love, we discover that our purpose is intricately tied to His divine plan for our lives.

In the pursuit of purpose and fulfillment, we often find ourselves seeking temporal things that can never truly satisfy our souls. However, when we anchor our lives in God's Love, we understand that our ultimate fulfillment comes from being in a deep, intimate relationship with Him. His Love fills the void within us, giving us a sense of wholeness and contentment that nothing else can provide.

Moreover, finding purpose and fulfillment in God's Love empowers us to impact the world around us. When we allow His Love to overflow from our hearts, it radiates through our actions, words, and relationships. Our ferocious passion for God becomes contagious, drawing others closer to Him and inspiring them to seek their own purpose in His Love.

Living a life centered on God's Love also brings clarity and direction to every aspect of our existence. It helps us navigate through the challenges and uncertainties of life, knowing that we are held securely in His embrace. In times of doubt or confusion, we can rely on His Love to guide us, giving us the confidence to pursue our purpose with unwavering faith.

In conclusion, finding purpose and fulfillment in God's Love is the key to living a life of ferocious passion for Him. It is through His Love that we discover our true purpose, experience deep fulfillment, and impact the world around us. Let us, as believers who love the Lord, embrace His Love with fervor and allow it to overflow into every aspect of our lives.Allowing Ferocious Love to Shape our Identity

In the pursuit of a deeper connection with our Creator, believers who love the Lord often find themselves yearning for a love that is not only passionate, but also ferocious. This intense affection, which stems from a place of complete surrender to God's Love, has the power to transform our lives and shape our very identity.

Ferocious Love is not a timid or lukewarm emotion; it is a powerful force that compels us to love God with an unrivaled intensity and fervor. It is a love that cannot be contained or restrained, but instead overflows and impacts every aspect of our existence. When we allow this ferocious Love to shape our identity, we become vessels through which God's Love can flow freely, touching the lives of those around us.

To embrace ferocious Love is to surrender our own desires and ambitions at the feet of our Creator. It requires us to let go of the things that hinder us from experiencing the fullness of His Love and to place Him at the center of our hearts and minds. When we do this, we find that our identity is no longer defined by the world, but by our intimate relationship with God.

Allowing ferocious Love to shape our identity means that we no longer conform to the patterns of this world, but are transformed by the renewing of our minds. We begin to see ourselves as God sees us – beloved children, chosen and set apart for a divine purpose. Our thoughts, actions, and decisions are guided by this deep Love, leading us to live lives that reflect the character of our Heavenly Father.

This ferocious Love also empowers us to love others with a radical compassion and grace. It enables us to see beyond the surface and embrace the brokenness and imperfections of those around us, just as God has embraced ours. As believers who love the Lord, we become conduits of His Love, spreading it to every corner of our lives and impacting the world around us.

In conclusion, embracing ferocious Love is not for the faint of heart. It requires a boldness and a willingness to surrender everything to God. However, the rewards are immeasurable. Allowing ferocious Love to shape our identity allows us to experience a depth of connection with our Creator that transcends human understanding. It transforms us into vessels of His Love, enabling us to impact the world around us in profound and meaningful ways. May we, as believers who love the Lord, embrace this ferocious Love and allow it to shape every aspect of our lives.

CHAPTER 9

LIVING A LIFE OF FEROCIOUS LOVE

～

Embracing a Lifestyle of Worship

In a world filled with distractions and busyness, it is essential for believers who love the Lord to embrace a lifestyle of Worship. This subchapter delves into the concept of living a life that is constantly devoted to worshiping God with intense passion and fervor. It explores the idea of allowing His Love to overflow and impact every aspect of life, leading to a life of purpose, joy, and fulfillment.

Worship is not limited to a Sunday morning church service or a specific time set aside for prayer. It is a way of life, a constant posture of the heart that acknowledges and exalts the greatness and goodness of God. When we embrace a lifestyle of Worship, we invite the presence of God into our lives and open ourselves up to His transformative power.

Ferocious Love is the driving force behind this lifestyle of Worship. It is a deep, intense affection for God that propels us to go beyond the surface level of religious rituals and traditions. It compels us to seek a genuine, intimate relationship with our Creator, where His Love becomes the very essence of who we are.

When we live a lifestyle of Worship, every moment becomes an opportunity to connect with God. Whether we are at work, spending time with family, or even doing mundane tasks, we can cultivate an awareness of God's presence and offer our thoughts, actions, and words as acts of Worship.

This lifestyle of Worship also extends to our relationships with others. As we overflow with God's Love, we become instruments of His grace and mercy, loving others with the same ferocious passion we have for God. Our relationships become a reflection of His Love, drawing others closer to Him.

Embracing a lifestyle of Worship requires intentional effort and a commitment to prioritizing God above all else. It means making time for prayer, studying His Word, and seeking opportunities to serve others. It means surrendering our desires, dreams, and ambitions to Him, trusting that His plans are far greater than our own.

In conclusion, embracing a lifestyle of Worship is not a one-time decision but an ongoing journey. It is a daily choice to love God with ferocious passion and allow His Love to overflow and impact every aspect of our lives. As believers who love the Lord, let us pursue this lifestyle of Worship, knowing that it is in His presence that we find true joy, fulfillment, and an unshakable purpose. Pursuing a Heart of Compassion

In the journey of loving God with ferocious passion, one cannot ignore the vital role of compassion. Compassion, the ability to empathize and feel the pain of others, is not just a desirable trait but an essential aspect of a believer's character.

As believers who love the Lord, we are called to imitate Jesus Christ, who was the epitome of compassion. His heart overflowed with Love and concern for the broken, the lost, and the marginalized. He touched lives and transformed them through acts of compassion, preaching the word, healing the sick, feeding the hungry, and comforting the sorrowful.

When we pursue a heart of compassion, we allow God's Love to overflow in our lives and impact every aspect of it. Compassion compels us to step outside our comfort zones and reach out to those in need, irrespective of their backgrounds, beliefs, or social status. It breaks down barriers and builds bridges, creating a space for understanding, healing, and restoration.

Compassion is not just a feeling; it is a call to action. It moves us to respond to the needs around us, to be the hands and feet of Jesus in a broken world. It prompts us to show kindness, offer help, and be a source of hope and encouragement to those who are hurting.

Pursuing a heart of compassion requires intentionality and a willingness to put others before ourselves. It means being sensitive to the needs of those around us, whether it be a family member, a neighbor, or a stranger we meet on the street. It means taking the time to listen, to understand, and to offer a helping hand.

In our pursuit of a heart of compassion, we must also remember to extend grace and forgiveness, just as Christ has done for us. We live in a world where people make mistakes, hurt one another, and fall short of expectations. Compassion allows us to see beyond the flaws and shortcomings, to offer second chances, and to walk alongside others in their journey of healing and restoration.

As believers who love the Lord, let us be known not only for our fervent passion but also for our compassionate hearts. May our Love for God overflow and impact every aspect of our lives, transforming us into vessels of His Love and instruments of His peace. May we pursue a heart of compassion, imitating our Savior and bringing hope to a hurting world. Radiating God's Love to the World

In the journey of loving God with ferocious passion, believers who truly love the Lord understand that their Love for Him should not be confined within the walls of their hearts. Instead, it should radiate outwards, reaching every corner of the world. This subchapter, "Radiating God's Love to the World," explores the transformative power of allowing His Love to overflow and impact every aspect of life.

As believers, we are called to be beacons of God's Love in a world desperate for hope and compassion. Our Love for God should be so intense and fervent that it cannot be contained. Just as the sun radiates light, we are to radiate God's Love to those around us. It is not a passive love, but an active and intentional choice to reflect His character.

Radiating God's Love starts with a genuine desire to see His love manifest in our lives. It is a willingness to surrender our own desires and priorities, allowing His Love to permeate every decision we make. This means embracing humility, forgiveness, and kindness as we interact with others. It means seeing people through God's eyes and recognizing their inherent worth and value.

To radiate God's Love effectively, believers must also be intentional about seeking opportunities to serve and bless others. Whether it is through acts of kindness, volunteering, or sharing the Gospel, we are called to be the hands and feet of Jesus in a broken world. By demonstrating His Love in tangible ways, we become living examples of His grace and mercy.

Furthermore, radiating God's Love requires us to break free from the limitations of our comfort zones. It means stepping out in faith to share His Love with those who may be different from us, those who are hurting, or even those who have wronged us. When we choose to love unconditionally, without expecting anything in return, we become channels of His Love that transform lives and bring healing to broken hearts.

Ultimately, radiating God's Love to the world is not just a noble endeavor; it is a commandment from our Savior Himself. Jesus said, "A new command I give you: Love one another. As I have loved you, so you must love one another" (John 13:34). When we truly grasp the depth of His Love for us, we cannot help but share it with others. The greatest act of Love is to preach the Gospel; when we preach the word, we are literally rescuing people from hell, bringing them from darkness into the light of God's word. All of these things are a byproduct of loving God and being loved by God.

Believers who love the Lord with ferocious passion understand that God's Love is not meant to be contained or hoarded, but to be shared generously. It is a love that transcends boundaries and transforms lives. As we allow His Love to overflow in every aspect of our lives, we become catalysts for change, bringing hope, joy, and restoration to a world in desperate need.

CHAPTER 10

THE ETERNAL IMPACT OF FEROCIOUS LOVE

~

Leaving a Legacy of Ferocious Love

In the pursuit of intense affection and fervent Love for God, believers who love the Lord often find themselves compelled to leave a lasting legacy. This legacy is not one of material possessions or worldly accomplishments but rather a testament to the transformative power of ferocious Love. It is a legacy that impacts every aspect of life, forever changing the lives of those who encounter it.

To leave a legacy of ferocious Love, one must fully embrace the concept of loving God with intense passion and fervor. This means going beyond mere religious rituals and devoting oneself wholeheartedly to a deep, personal relationship with the Creator. It entails allowing His Love to overflow from within and permeate every area of life - from relationships and work to hobbies and dreams.

When we love God with ferocious passion, we become vessels of His Love, radiating it to those around us. Our actions, words, and attitudes become infused with the transformative power of God's divine affection, his agape. We become conduits for His Love to touch the lives of others, leaving a lasting impact that goes far beyond our own existence.

Leaving a legacy of ferocious Love requires embracing a radical shift in mindset and lifestyle. It means prioritizing the eternal over the temporary and investing in things of eternal significance. It means choosing to love sacrificially, without expecting anything in return. It means extending grace and forgiveness even when it is difficult. It means living a life marked by compassion, kindness, and selflessness.

As believers who love the Lord, we have the opportunity to leave a legacy that transcends our earthly limitations. We can choose to embrace the call to love God with ferocious passion, allowing His Love to flow through us and impact the lives of those we encounter. Our legacy can be one of transformation, healing, and restoration - a testament to the power of divine affection.

In conclusion, leaving a legacy of ferocious Love is the pinnacle of loving God with intense passion and fervor. It is a legacy that impacts every aspect of life, transforming the lives of those who encounter it. As believers who love the Lord, we have the power to leave a legacy that will endure long after we are gone. Let us embrace the call to love God with ferocious passion and allow His Love to overflow, leaving a legacy of transformative Love for generations to come. Experiencing Eternal Union with God's Love

In the depths of our souls, believers who love the Lord yearn for a profound and unbreakable connection with our Creator. We long to experience a love that transcends all earthly boundaries, a love that is eternal and unchanging. This subchapter, "Experiencing Eternal Union with God's Love," delves into the depths of this divine connection, exploring how we can cultivate a ferocious passion for God and allow His Love to overflow into every aspect of our lives.

To truly understand the concept of eternal union with God's Love, we must first grasp the immense depth and magnitude of His Love for us. It is a love that surpasses all understanding, a love that was demonstrated through the sacrifice of His Son, Jesus Christ, on the cross. This divine Love has the power to transform our lives, if only we open our hearts and allow it to do so.

In order to experience this eternal union, we must approach our relationship with God with a ferocious love and passion. It requires a fervent devotion and an unwavering commitment to seeking His presence in every moment of our lives. We must hunger and thirst for righteousness, desiring to know God intimately and intimately, knowing His Love for us.

Practically, experiencing eternal union with God's Love means surrendering our will to His and aligning our desires with His desires. It means spending intentional time in prayer and meditation, allowing His Spirit to speak to us and guide our thoughts and actions. It means immersing ourselves in His Word, studying and meditating on the truths found within its pages.

As believers who love the Lord, we must also learn to let His love overflow into every aspect of our lives. We must allow His Love to shape our relationships, our work, and our daily interactions. It means extending His Love and grace to others, even when it's difficult. It means being a vessel through which His Love can touch and transform the lives of those around us.

Experiencing eternal union with God's Love is not a one-time event but an ongoing journey. It requires constant cultivation and nurturing of our relationship with God. As we seek Him with a ferocious love and allow His Love to overflow, we will find ourselves transformed from the inside out. Our lives will be marked by an intense affection for God, and His Love will radiate through us, impacting everyone we encounter.

In conclusion, "Experiencing Eternal Union with God's Love" is an invitation to believers who love the Lord to pursue a deep and unbreakable connection with our Creator. It encourages us to cultivate a ferocious passion for God, allowing His Love to overflow and impact every aspect of our lives. Through intentional devotion, surrender, and a willingness to let His Love shape us, we can truly experience eternal union with God's Love, forever transformed by His grace and presence.

Celebrating the Rewards of Ferocious Love

Subchapter: Celebrating the Rewards of Ferocious Love

In this subchapter, we embark on a journey to explore the incredible rewards and blessings that await those who choose to embrace the concept of ferocious Love - the art of loving God with intense passion and fervor. This chapter is dedicated to all believers who love the Lord and are seeking a deeper, more fulfilling relationship with Him.

When we truly grasp the essence of ferocious Love and allow it to permeate every aspect of our lives, we open ourselves up to a world of remarkable rewards. One of the first rewards we experience is an overwhelming sense of joy and fulfillment. Loving God with such intensity brings us a profound sense of purpose and contentment that cannot be found anywhere else. Our hearts overflow with gratitude and awe as we witness the transformative power of His Love in our lives.

Furthermore, ferocious Love has the potential to impact every area of our existence. As we surrender ourselves to this passionate love affair with God, we begin to see His Love radiate through us, influencing our relationships, careers, and even our daily interactions. Our Love for God becomes contagious, inspiring those around us to seek Him and experience the same incredible rewards.

Additionally, ferocious Love grants us an unshakable faith and unwavering confidence in God's promises.

Through the trials and tribulations of life, our intense Love for Him becomes an anchor, keeping us grounded and steadfast. We find comfort and strength in knowing that He is always with us, guiding and protecting us every step of the way.

Moreover, celebrating the rewards of ferocious Love also means being open to the supernatural manifestations of God's blessings. As we pour out our Love for Him, He pours out His blessings upon us in ways we cannot comprehend. Doors of opportunity swing wide open, miracles become a regular occurrence, and divine favor becomes our constant companion.

Ultimately, celebrating the rewards of ferocious Love is an invitation to a life beyond our wildest dreams. It is an invitation to experience the depths of God's Love and to witness the extraordinary impact it can have on our lives and the lives of those around us. So let us embrace this concept with open hearts and minds, allowing God's ferocious Love to overflow within us and transform us into vessels of His glorious Love.

Milton Keynes UK
Ingram Content Group UK Ltd.
UKHW020737291223
435170UK00014B/461